This book is dedicated to my brother James S. Ross Sr., for reaching back to pull me forward.

This book is also dedicated to Priscilla Edwards for your sense of wonder and many whys.

Me on the Page Publishing
Copyright © 2022 Phelicia Lang M.Ed.

ISBN-13: 979-8-9855827-4-1

This book is sold subject to the condition that it shall not, by way of trade or otherwise, be lent, resold, hired out or otherwise circulated without the publisher's prior consent in any form of binding or cover other than that in which it is published and without a similar condition including
this condition being imposed on the subsequent publisher.
The moral right of the author has been asserted.

Illustrations Copyright © Phelicia Lang M.Ed.

Illustrations by Samanta Veliz (Uzuri Designs)
& Henry Ezeokeke

Tay and Friends
Early Science Readers
By Phelicia Lang M.Ed.

Book 1

Reading Tips

Dear Family,

Our world is filled with many fun things to explore. Your child is filled with wonder and amazement of how things work. Cultivate their interest by reading great books and providing opportunities for them to think like a Scientist, Technologist, Engineer or Mathematician.

Little Scientist, you will need to use your non-fiction text skills as you navigate the pages.

I'm sure you will say 'Hey, that's Me on the pages!", as you make connections while reading about Tay and Friends.

Stay safe and Be Well,

Phelicia Lang

If your child gets stuck on a word...

Look at the picture	👀
Touch each letter and say its sound slowly	bag
Go back and re-read	⤴
Skip the word and come back to it	bag and
Go back and read it again	⤴

Remember to always think...

- Does my word make sense?
- Does my word look right?
- Does my word sound right?

Non-fiction Text Features in this Book	
Label A word next to a picture that identifies what it is.	
Keyword Important vocabulary words in the text that maybe bold, italics, or colored.	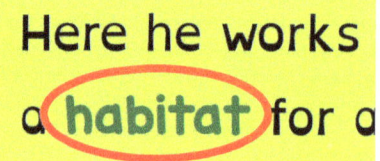
Glossary A page in near the back of the book where you can find the meanings of the keywords.	

Captions

A title or words underneath a picture that tells about the picture above it.

Tay
Goes to
STEM Camp

He loves to ask questions about how things work.

Tay is home for the summer and will go to **STEM** Camp.

STEM is a short way to say:

Science,
Technology,
Engineering and
Math.

What's inside an owl's pellet?

At **STEM** Camp he will be a scientist. Tay will ask lots of questions and work to find answers.

How does a ball bounce?

This is Raj.

He plays soccer with Tay. Raj's dad is a math teacher at the **STEM** Camp.

Tay sees his friend Aleeyah.

Her mom is a **science** teacher at **STEM** Camp.

He also sees his cousin Mari and his aunt.

Aunt Cee-Cee is an **Engineer** teacher at the **STEM** Camp.

Tuskegee University in Tuskegee, Alabama. It is a school where you can learn how to be an engineer.

He's excited and ready to get to work.

The **STEM** Camp looks like a big play room with four doors.

gears

First, they must learn the rules to be safe in the labs:

1. We are kind to each other and the **environment**
2. We are respectful with each other and our tools
3. We focus on having fun, in a safe way
4. We will listen before we act
5. We will follow all the rules inside and outside

Which animals are its enemies?

An egret in its habitat.

On day one they visit the **Science** room. Here he works to build a **habitat** for a bird.

What environment does it need?

How can it protect itself?

What does it eat?

On day two they visit the **Technology** room. Here they work to build a robot and to make it move.

What is a code?

dropper

Is it a gas?

Is it a solid?

On day three they enter the **Engineers** room. This is Tay's favorite because his Aunt Cee-Cee is there. Here they will find out why some chemicals change when mixed with others.

What is a dropper?

Is it a liquid?

What makes gears move?

How heavy is it?

What size is it?

On day four, they visit the **Math** room. Here they will use numbers to solve problems and to **measure**.

ruler

How far?

How long?

On day five Tay and his friends will share their projects with their families.

They put on lab coats and goggles. They show and share all the fun things they learned. The families clap and cheer.

They all had fun
at **STEM** camp.

Will they be Scientists?
Engineers?
Or Mathematicians?

They can be just what
they dream to be.

Just like Tay and Friends,
you can dream big dreams
and be kind too.

What will you be?

Glossary

Dropper: a short tube with a bulb on one end that is used to measure liquids.

Habitats: places where lots of living things live and work together.

Code: the way we tell computers to do the things they do.

Environment: the surroundings that people, animals and plants live in.

Solid: objects that are firm and keep their shape

Liquid: flowing like water

Gas: air-like substances that can move around freely, and take on the shape of its container.

Measure: a way to know the size, amount, or degree of something.

Engineer: a person who builds and designs things.

Technology: helps us to support the changes we make in our environment easier to use.

Science: ways to learn about our world by observing, and experimenting

Math: the study of numbers, shapes and measurements.

Gears: can be wheels and teeth that fit together to transfer force and motion.

About the Author

Phelicia is a loving wife to Tony, mother to four wonderful children, and precious grandchildren. They have all inspired her journey to find good books to reflect their lives and interests.

As a Reading Specialist she's passionate about finding the right books to help readers connect to stories they love and books that reflect the readers.

Dreaming big dreams and using those dreams and gifts to help others, is the message she shares with her students.

When she's not creating on her computer she can be found Dreaming Big Dreams, reading and shopping.

More Books by Phelicia Lang

Tay Book Series

Mari Book Series

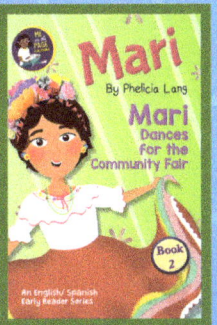

www.meonthepage.com

www.ingramcontent.com/pod-product-compliance
Lightning Source LLC
LaVergne TN
LVHW070524070526
838199LV00072B/6699